HEALTH WATCH

Epilepsy

Revised Edition

WITHDRAWN

MARK EDWARD DUDLEY

Expert Reviews by Susan Spencer, M.D.;
Patricia E. Gay, Ph.D.; and Laurie M.
Brown-Croyts, Ph.D.

Enslow Publishers, Inc.

40 Industrial Road   PO Box 38
Box 398   Aldershot
Berkeley Heights, NJ 07922   Hants GU12 6BP
USA   UK

http://www.enslow.com

Dedicated to Tamara Moxham.

Acknowledgments
With thanks to:
Susan Spencer, M.D., Department of Neurology, Yale School of Medicine, for her advice and review of this book.
Tamara Moxham and David Hall for their willingness to share their stories.

Printed in the United States of America. This is a revised edition of Epilepsy ©1997.

Library of Congress Cataloging-in-Publication Data
Dudley, Mark Edward.
    Epilepsy / Mark Edward Dudley—Rev. ed.
        p. cm. —— (Health watch)
Includes bibliographical references and index.
    ISBN 0-7660-1661-7 (hardcover: alk. paper)
    1. Epilepsy—Juvenile literature. [1. Epilepsy.
    2. Diseases.] I. Title. II. Health watch
(Berkeley Heights, N.J.)
        RC372.2.D83 2001
        616.8'53—dc21   00-010517
10 9 8 7 6 5 4 3 2 1

To Our Readers:
All Internet addresses in this book were active and appropriate when we went to press. Any comments or suggestions can be sent by e-mail to Comments@enslow.com or to the address on the back cover.

Illustration and Photo Credits:
© Brian Ruel: pp. 1, 4; courtesy, Tamara Moxham: p. 6; © Jill Gregory, p. 10; © Carl D. Walsh, pp. 13, 33; © PhotoDisc: p. 15; courtesy, Bio-logic Systems Corp. (© 2000 David Joel): p. 24; courtesy, National Institute of Neurological Disorders & Stroke (photos by William K. Geiger): pp. 25, 35; © Digital Stock, Corbis Corp.: p. 26 (*top*); courtesy, the Centre for PET, Austin & Repatriation Medical Centre, Melbourne, Australia: p. 26 (*bottom*); © John C. Gold: p. 38.

Cover Illustrations:
Large photo, courtesy, Bio-logic Systems Corp. (© 2000 David Joel); top inset, © Jill Gregory; bottom inset, © Brian Ruel.

Contents

Tamara Moxham hugs her little brother, Travers Dudley Ruel. Tamara, diagnosed with childhood epilepsy, has had no seizures since 1994.

Chapter 1

Tamara's Story

Tamara Moxham was confused. A moment before, the six-year-old girl had been perched on the trapeze on her friend's swing set. Now she was sitting on the ground bleeding. She couldn't recall falling or cutting her chin. Her friend called to her mother for help. The next thing Tamara knew, she was in the house, and someone was holding ice to her chin. She had no idea how she got there.

"There was no passage of time, as there is during sleep," Tamara recalled as an adult. She had simply blacked out for a few moments. Tamara didn't know what had happened to her that day until many years later. At the hospital, the doctor bandaged her chin but ignored her blackout. He thought Tamara had fallen because the trapeze was so narrow. The doctor didn't realize that something was wrong with Tamara's brain.

Tamara had epilepsy. Epilepsy is not a disease but a brain disorder that causes people to have **seizures**. It was a seizure that caused Tamara to black out. A seizure happens

Tamara Moxham in 1974 at age four.

when the electrical currents in the brain go out of control. If this happens to a person more than once or twice, with no definite reason for the attack, doctors conclude that the person has epilepsy. But not all seizures are the result of epilepsy. Sometimes drugs or high fever can cause a seizure. In those cases, if there is no permanent damage to the brain, the seizures will stop. People with epilepsy, however, may have seizures again and again. One person of every ten will have a seizure of some sort in his or her lifetime.

Seizures take on many forms. Tamara's was an **absence seizure**. When people have absence seizures, they often seem to be daydreaming. They may nod their heads or blink rapidly. Many times they don't even know that they've had an attack.

A **tonic-clonic seizure** is more severe. When people have these attacks, they lose control of their bodies and pass out. Their bodies stiffen and fall. Then they begin to jerk and shake. During these seizures some people may see or hear things that aren't there. They may smack their lips or say the same things over and over without realizing what they are doing.

Stress, poor diet, poor sleeping habits, drugs, or flashing lights can trigger attacks. Seizures can occur in newborn babies, children, teenagers, adults, and the elderly. People can be asleep or awake during a seizure. Animals can get epilepsy, too. The condition can get steadily worse or vanish altogether. Epilepsy can be a minor bother, or it can be a life-threatening disorder. Most people will never have another seizure if they take the proper medicines. Other people will need to wear protective gear to keep themselves from getting hurt during seizures.

In up to 70 percent of epilepsy cases, there is no known cause. This is especially true in childhood cases. Doctors call this idiopathic or cryptogenic epilepsy. Those with **idiopathic epilepsy** have the best chance of recovery. This is the type of epilepsy that Tamara Moxham had. Her doctors could find nothing wrong with her brain that would explain her attacks. Tamara later learned that she was probably born with epilepsy.

But Tamara is one of the lucky ones. The form of epilepsy that she had is known as childhood epilepsy. People with this type of epilepsy often stop having attacks after they reach their mid-twenties. Tamara has had no seizures for six years, since she was twenty-four years old.

Aside from attention deficit disorder, epilepsy is the most common brain disorder in children and the third most common in adults after stroke and **Alzheimer's disease**. More than two million people in the United States have epilepsy. Half of those people developed epilepsy by age ten. More than three hundred thousand children aged fourteen years and younger have epilepsy. Nearly one adult in ten has a close relative with epilepsy. Three percent of people living to the age of seventy-five will develop epilepsy sometime during their lives. Such a widespread illness deserves a closer look.

Chapter 2

Causes of Epilepsy

Epilepsy is one of the oldest known health disorders. Scientists have found signs of epilepsy in people who lived thirty thousand years ago. Hammurabi, king of Babylon around 1800 B.C., described epileptic attacks. The first scientific writings on the condition were done in ancient Greece. The name *epilepsy* comes from the Greek word *epilambanein,* meaning "to seize upon."

Many ancient peoples believed that evil spirits caused seizures. Superstitious people spat on people having seizures to keep the spirits away. This was so common that people called epilepsy the "spitting disease."

The Romans thought epilepsy was merely another of the countless sicknesses plaguing humanity. The famous Greek doctor Galen, who lived in Rome during the second century, was the first to describe the **aura**. This is a sensation some people feel just before a seizure begins. Doctors still use this term today. One of Galen's patients described the feeling as a cool breeze inside his body. *Aura* is the Greek word for "breeze."

During the Middle Ages, many people believed that only a saint could cure people with epilepsy. Some thought that if they looked at a person having an epileptic attack, they would be possessed by demons. Even those who believed epilepsy was a disease thought it was contagious. They thought the breath or saliva of people with epilepsy was poisonous. Some doctors thought moonlight caused epilepsy.

Authorities kept people with epilepsy apart from others. People with epilepsy were isolated in hospitals and insane asylums. Most people believed that those with epilepsy were crazy. Only fifty years ago, thousands of people with epilepsy remained locked in mental institutions.

Research and the Brain

Gradually, attitudes about epilepsy began to change. In the eighteenth century Thomas Beddoes, an English doctor, suggested that anyone could get epilepsy. Beddoes and others worked to have patients with epilepsy released from insane asylums.

Dr. Hughlings Jackson, who was also from England, did a great deal of research on epilepsy. For forty years, beginning in 1862, he published the results of his research. Jackson described a seizure as "an occasional, sudden, massive, rapid, and local discharge of the gray matter," which is a part of the brain. He had good reason to study epilepsy so thoroughly—his wife had the disorder.

In the 1920s, a German doctor, Hans Berger, created a device that could record **brain waves**. Doctors later called the machine an **electroencephalograph**. It works by

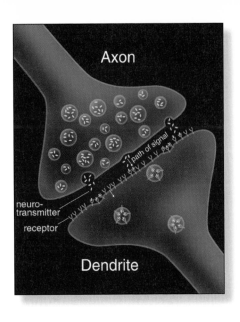

Axon

neuro-
transmitter

receptor

Dendrite

sensing the minute electrical fields of nerve cells in the brain. Berger noticed that the brain waves of people with epilepsy looked strange just before a seizure. He showed that the type of seizure sometimes could be predicted by noting which area of the brain had an odd pattern.

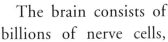

The transmission of a signal between cells.

The brain consists of billions of nerve cells, called **neurons**. Neurons send messages between the brain and the body through nerves. Some neurons transmit messages to the brain from the sense organs, such as the eyes, ears, and skin. Other neurons send orders from the brain to the muscles.

Neurons have **dendrites** on one end and **axons** on the other. When something stimulates a dendrite, an electric current flows to the axon. The axon then gives off a chemical called a **neurotransmitter**. This in turn stimulates the dendrite of the next neuron in line.

As the brain works, its neurons give off electric signals in regular patterns. These signals can be detected by a device called an electroencephalograph, just as a radio detects the signals emitted by a radio station. The electroencephalograph records the neurons' signals—called brain waves—as wavy lines on paper. Doctors can then study this recording, known as an **electroencephalogram (EEG)**.

Doctors can tell a lot about how the brain works from looking at an electroencephalogram. They cannot read a person's thoughts, but they can tell whether he or she is asleep or awake, calm or excited. They can also tell when the brain is acting normally and when it isn't. Soon after the EEG's invention, doctors found that people with epilepsy produce unusual brain waves. In most cases the doctors could tell this even when the person had no symptoms. And during a seizure, the doctors could plainly see the person's brain waves were out of control.

We now know that during a seizure, many neurons fire at once, over and over. The trouble can begin in a small part of the brain. The faulty neurons send signals to neighboring cells. This causes them to fire, too. The effect spreads until it involves a large part of the brain. The normal business of the brain shuts down. Talking, standing, remembering, and even breathing sometimes become impossible. Eventually, the electrical "storm" dies down, and the brain returns to normal.

On the other hand, many seizures involve the whole brain from the beginning. How a person looks or feels during a seizure can show where a seizure starts and indicate whether it begins in a small part of the brain or the whole brain.

Known Causes of Epilepsy

Doctors do not know what causes epilepsy in up to 70 percent of those who have it. Some of these people have inherited the tendency to have seizures. This is true in many of those who have childhood epilepsy. In the other

30 percent, epilepsy can be traced to a disease, injury, or other factor. This type of epilepsy is called **symptomatic epilepsy**. About 43 percent of people with symptomatic epilepsy were born with it. Sometimes this happens because a sickness the mother had while she was pregnant damaged the brain of the fetus. Measles is one disease that can do this. Drugs, poisons, or radiation can also affect pregnant women and harm an unborn child's brain. If the mother has a difficult delivery, sometimes the baby can't breathe right away. This can also lead to brain damage and epilepsy.

Childhood diseases are another leading cause of symptomatic epilepsy. About 27 percent of symptomatic epilepsy cases are caused by infectious diseases. Tuberculosis, meningitis, and measles can all cause epilepsy.

Almost 5 percent of all young children at some point develop fevers that trigger convulsions. These are called febrile seizures. Recent research shows that these seizures may occasionally make the brain more prone to epilepsy later in life.

Among adults, head injuries are the leading known cause of epilepsy. They account for about 17 percent of all symptomatic epilepsy cases. Head injuries are often the result of sports or automobile accidents. Many of these injuries can be prevented.

One person who developed epilepsy from a head injury is David Hall. David fell off his bicycle when he was nine years old. Years later, he began having seizures. He cautions children to wear protective headgear while riding bikes. "Tomorrow can be a hard day to approach with a brain injury," he warns.

As adults get older they face an increasing danger of getting epilepsy. Ten percent of people in nursing homes are being treated with antiseizure medications. One hazard to the elderly is brain tumors. About one-third of all brain tumors result in epilepsy.

Strokes can also lead to epilepsy. A stroke happens when a blood vessel in the brain bursts or is blocked. Stroke victims are twenty-two times more likely than

David Hall stands next to the tractor he uses to do landscaping work. He has had epilepsy since he was injured in a bicycle accident at age nine.

others to develop epilepsy. Alzheimer's disease is another illness that affects the brain. People who have Alzheimer's are ten times more likely to have epilepsy than those who do not have the disease. Brain defects also can cause epilepsy.

Other diseases can sometimes increase a person's chances of getting epilepsy. For instance, diabetes causes sugar in the blood to rise far above normal. If the sugar level is not brought down, the brain can be affected, causing epilepsy. Environmental poisons can have the same effect. Children who eat lead-based paint are at risk of developing epilepsy. So are those who have a bad response to certain medicines or to bee stings. Those who abuse alcohol or drugs are also more likely to develop epilepsy.

Mumps or measles can increase the chances of having epilepsy but only in rare cases.

About 15 percent of those with epilepsy pass on some risk to their children. Scientists are trying to find the genes responsible for these cases. To do this, doctors test many members of families in which epilepsy is common. They compare the deoxyribonucleic acid (DNA) of family members with and without epilepsy. Differences provide clues to which genes control the traits that lead to epilepsy. DNA is a molecule inside the body that carries the genetic code for each person. It determines a person's traits, such as eye color and height and can also determine who will have a tendency to get certain diseases or disorders.

These studies will help scientists to develop genetic tests. Such tests will allow early diagnosis of some types of epilepsy. Family members who show no symptoms can be tested, too. People will know the chances of passing epilepsy on to their children. Knowing which genes are involved will also tell doctors more about the causes of epilepsy and may someday lead to a cure.

Conditions That Trigger Seizures

For some people with epilepsy, certain conditions seem to trigger seizures. These conditions are referred to as **precipitants**. Stress or lack of sleep may lead to a seizure. David Hall had a seizure once after working all night as part of a fire crew. Doctors sometimes ask patients to stay awake the night before their examinations. This makes it easier to detect epilepsy with an EEG.

Tamara Moxham developed an eating disorder during

college that made her more susceptible to seizures. Because she forced herself to vomit, her epilepsy medication didn't stay in her body long enough to keep the seizures under control.

Colds, infections, and other common illnesses increase the chances of a seizure in people who have epilepsy. Cold pills, alcohol, and other drugs may do the same. David Hall tells of the time he drank punch at a wedding, unaware that it had alcohol in it. Soon after, he had a seizure.

Mental stress can be as bad as physical stress for those with epilepsy. Fretting about a date or a test at school may trigger a seizure. Loud, annoying, or repetitive music can do the same. Even a bad mood can cause an attack. The minor problems of everyday life are more apt to set someone off than major, life-changing events. For some people, the best way to prevent a seizure is to rest quietly in a darkened room. Others can ward off seizures by concentrating on breathing normally during stressful times.

Many people with epilepsy are photosensitive, or sensitive to light or patterns of light. This sensitivity can cause them to have a seizure. Staring too long at video games, checkerboard designs, flickering television screens, or neon signs can cause seizures. Strobe lights are a problem for those who are photosensitive. Since many emergency vehicles use these

Strobe lights from an ambulance can trigger a seizure in some people with epilepsy.

lights, drivers or observers of these vehicles have an increased chance of having a seizure if they have epilepsy.

Tamara discovered she was photosensitive in college when she was studying to become an interpreter for the deaf. "I went to college with about two thousand deaf people," she said. "Since they use strobe lights for fire alarms and doorbells, I began to have tonic-clonic seizures."

Doctors don't know how seizures start or spread through the brain. Some think that people have repeated seizures because the brain memorizes them. When electrical signals travel a certain pathway, it becomes easier for those neurons to carry the same signal next time. This is how we learn to do repetitive tasks. The brain may "learn" seizures in the same way. Doctors call this process **kindling**. Even though many of the causes of epilepsy remain a mystery, doctors have learned a great deal about its processes and effects. They are often able to control seizures with treatment.

Chapter 3

Types of Seizures

Tamara Moxham was twenty years old before she realized she had epilepsy. Looking back, she now recognizes the signs from her teen years. There were times in school when she was confused because it seemed as if the teacher had skipped part of the lesson.

As Tamara got older, her symptoms got worse. "I would notice that the show on television that I had been watching was suddenly near the end, or that the music I was listening to seemed to skip. Once it happened while I was looking at a clock. The hands seemed to jump several minutes ahead in front of my eyes."

Absence seizures like the ones Tamara experienced are common among young people with epilepsy. These spells usually last just seconds. In most cases they are harmless. But if they happen while a person is driving or performing a similar task, they can be dangerous. David Hall once hit two gas pumps with his car during an attack. His epilepsy is now under control with medication.

There are more than thirty types of epileptic seizures.

These are divided into two categories: generalized and **partial seizures**.

Generalized Seizures

Generalized seizures affect the whole brain and almost always cause those having a seizure to lose consciousness. About half of all cases of epilepsy involve generalized seizures. Absence seizures are an example of this type of seizure. There are several types of generalized seizures. In some of these, a person will lose consciousness for only seconds. In others, a person may be unconscious for several minutes.

An **akinetic seizure**, which is similar to an absence seizure, affects the ability of a person to walk, run, or move in other ways. The attacks occur when a person is moving. During the attack, the person stops moving for a few seconds and then starts moving again, not knowing that the movements were interrupted.

More serious are **atonic seizures** or drop attacks. These seizures make the muscles relax. The person having the attack slumps and falls to the floor. This type of seizure is rare and can occur with akinetic seizures.

A **myoclonic seizure** causes muscles to jerk. Symptoms may be as mild as a shaking leg, or they can be so violent that they cause a person to fall to the ground. This happens most often in the morning. Myoclonic and absence seizures are often idiopathic. This type of epilepsy is more apt to run in families.

Tonic-clonic seizures are the most common type of generalized seizure. They happen in two stages. In the **tonic**

phase, muscles contract and the whole body becomes rigid and falls. The seizure forces air from the lungs. Often this causes the person to emit a loud cry. During this kind of seizure, people pass out.

The **clonic phase** follows. The muscles alternately contract and relax, causing the person to shake and thrash around. During this phase, some people may lose control of their bowels. They may bite their tongues or stop breathing. The jerking may last for seconds or for several minutes. Then they relax and regain consciousness. This is known as the post-ictal phase. Often they are confused for a short time after an attack. They may fall asleep afterward. Sometimes a person who has had an attack suffers from sore muscles, nausea, or a headache. These symptoms usually last for a few minutes, though sometimes they can continue for a week or so.

Doctors once called tonic-clonic attacks grand mal seizures. *Grand mal* is French for "great illness." Absence attacks were known as petit mal ("little illness") seizures. These were the first two types of epilepsy to be described.

One person with tonic-clonic seizures described an attack in this way:

> "[It was] just like a sudden thunder and lightning storm. Every part of the brain rushed to [fight the storm]. The brain was so busy working to [deal with] the storm that it couldn't do the rest of the things it usually did, such as making the arms and legs work. In fact, the brain got so busy trying to [deal with] the storm, it forgot all about sending messages to

the rest of the body, so the body didn't know what to do, and just twitched and jerked around for awhile, until the thunder and lightning storm [ended]. Then the brain went back to doing its usual job, except it was really tired from all the work and just wanted to take a nap for awhile."

Partial Seizures

Another type of epilepsy involves partial seizures. These are also called local or focal seizures. These seizures begin in a specific area of the brain. Often these areas are the site of a brain injury. Symptoms of a partial seizure depend on the **focal point**, or the part of the brain where the seizure starts. A person having a **simple partial seizure** stays conscious during the attack. The four basic types of simple partial seizures are motor, sensory, autonomic, and psychic.

A partial seizure that affects only the muscles is called a **motor seizure**. The muscles may twitch or jerk many times. One type of motor seizure is called **Jacksonian epilepsy**, after Hughlings Jackson, an English doctor who studied epilepsy in the nineteenth century. A Jacksonian seizure starts at a place in the brain that controls motor movement. As it spreads, more muscles become involved. Such a seizure often begins in a finger as a tingling or trembling. The tingling or trembling then moves up the arm. Jackson's wife had this type of epilepsy.

A partial seizure that affects the part of the brain controlling the senses is called a **sensory seizure**. If a seizure begins in the occipital cortex, which controls the eyes, a person may see shapes and colors that aren't really there. Seizures in the **auditory cortex**, which controls hearing, may cause a person to imagine sounds.

An **autonomic seizure**—one in the **autonomic nervous system**, which regulates the body's automatic functions—may affect digestion, heartbeat, or breathing. **Psychic seizures** may not affect the body but may alter one's emotions. The person may feel rage, panic, or fear.

About 30 percent of all epilepsy cases are **complex partial seizures**. Often these attacks begin in one part of the brain and then spread to the **temporal lobes**. This part of the brain controls thoughts and emotions. In many cases, the attacks, often called temporal lobe attacks, affect both muscles and thought processes. In the past, doctors called these psychomotor seizures. People having these attacks behave strangely. They may repeat simple tasks, such as adjusting their clothes over and over. They may repeat the same words or phrases, or wander aimlessly. They may feel intense emotions. If the seizure involves the area of the brain controlling memory, a person may recall vivid scenes.

People who have complex partial seizures may appear to know what they are doing. But, they are really in a dream-like state. After the attack, they recall little of what happened. Others may think that a person having the seizure is crazy or is taking illegal drugs. The parent of one child with epilepsy laments, "I wish he just had tonic-clonic [seizures]. Everyone can understand them instead of these complex partial seizures where he walks around, snapping his fingers. It looks so odd. Nobody knows what he's doing." Both simple and complex seizures can spread to affect the whole brain. The person having the seizure may then lose consciousness. Tonic-clonic seizures sometimes start this way. Doctors call seizures that spread in this way **secondarily generalized seizures**.

A partial seizure may begin with an aura, which is actually a mild form of simple partial seizure. The way that people experience an aura depends on where in the brain the seizure begins. Muscles may feel tingly. The person may smell something strange. There may be a feeling of unreality.

An aura can be helpful. It gives the person time to lie down or alert others that an attack is on the way. Most seizures aren't dangerous by themselves. Injuries occur when a person falls down or has a seizure in a dangerous situation. Usually there are no lasting ill effects even if a person stops breathing for a time during a seizure. After the seizure passes, body functions restart automatically.

Some people have **pseudo seizures** that are caused by psychological disorders, not epilepsy or brain damage. The symptoms are similar to epileptic seizures. The only way to be sure if a person has epilepsy is by administering an EEG during a seizure. About 20 percent of patients who don't respond to treatment for epilepsy have pseudo seizures.

Status epilepticus occurs when a person has many seizures in a row that do not stop. People can die from this condition because it exhausts the body and the brain. Also, a person in this state may stop breathing and not get enough oxygen to the brain. Status epilepticus most often occurs when patients stop taking their epilepsy drugs. It is important for recovering patients to stop their medication gradually. They should always follow their doctor's orders.

Chapter 4

Diagnosis

Epilepsy is not always easy to identify. Headaches and muscle spasms occur for many reasons. Everyone "spaces out" once in a while. Parents and teachers can easily confuse absence seizures with daydreaming. Temporal lobe seizures sometimes resemble mental illness or the symptoms of drug abuse. Heat exhaustion, infections, and many other illnesses that are not related to epilepsy can cause seizures.

Tamara Moxham finally sought help after a friend saw her fall down. A doctor at the hospital checked Tamara's blood and urine. He listened to her heart. Nothing was wrong. He thought she was imagining things. He sent her to a **neurologist** to be sure. A neurologist treats diseases of the brain and nervous system.

The neurologist connected Tamara to an electroencephalograph. A nurse taped twenty-five metal disks called electrodes to her head. Wires ran from the electrodes to the electroencephalograph. The doctor tested her brain waves with her eyes open and then with them closed. He

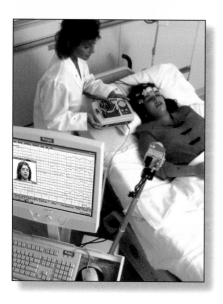

A technician connects a woman to an electro-encephalograph to measure her brain waves.

asked her to breathe in a different rhythm. He flashed strobe lights into her eyes. The doctor waited until Tamara fell asleep and recorded her brain waves again.

The doctor looked at the brain waves recorded by the electrodes. The brain waves were unusual, especially those recorded after Tamara breathed rapidly. Based on the results of the EEG readings and other tests, the doctor told Tamara she had epilepsy. He gave her a drug to control the seizures. As long as she took her medicine regularly, Tamara's seizures were less frequent and less severe.

Tests Tell the Story

An electroencephalogram will usually reveal whether a person has epilepsy. But even if a patient has normal results from an EEG, it doesn't rule out epilepsy. If there are other symptoms, the doctor may give a patient a **computerized axial tomography (CAT)** scan. A CAT scan works like an x-ray machine. It takes pictures of segments of the brain, as if the brain had been sliced into sections. A computer then uses the pictures to create a three-dimensional model of the brain.

During the test, a patient lies quietly on a bed with his

or her head in the machine. There is no pain or other sensation. The CAT scan shows whether anything is unusual in the brain. It may reveal scars from an old head injury, a clue that the patient has epilepsy. It also shows bleeding caused by a stroke.

Another test that doctors use when checking for epilepsy is called **magnetic resonance imaging (MRI)**. In an MRI scan, the brain is exposed to a magnetic field. A computer records the brain's response. The MRI scan gives a sharper picture of the brain than the CAT scan does. A new test called a **magnetoencephalogram (MEG)** records the natural magnetic fields of the brain.

In cases that are hard to diagnose, the doctor may decide to examine the patient's brain with a **positron emission tomography (PET)** scan. MRI and CAT scans show still pictures. The PET scan shows the brain in action. Because these tests are very expensive, doctors call for PET scans only when other methods don't answer their questions about the patient's condition.

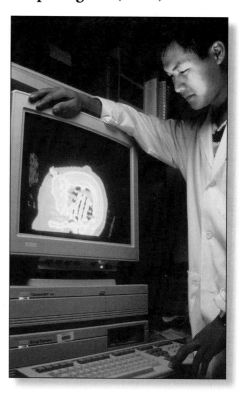

The screen shows the brain of a person with epilepsy.

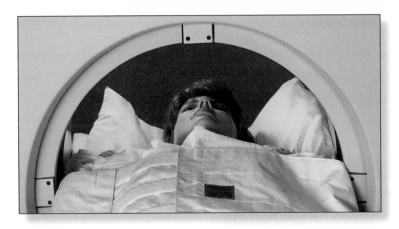

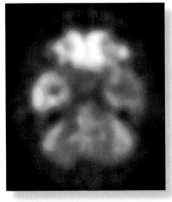

Above, a woman has a PET scan. At right, a PET-scan image of the brain of a patient with partial epilepsy shows reduced activity on the left side of the brain (right side of the picture). The image was taken between seizures. During a seizure, this area would show increased activity.

Some medical centers use another machine called a **single photon emission computed tomography (SPECT)** scan, which helps pinpoint the focal points of seizures.

Sometimes a doctor can tell where a seizure originates simply by watching the patient. To do this, doctors use video EEG monitoring/telemetry. One doctor who uses this technique is Dr. Christoph Baumgartner. He found that he could predict the affected area of the brain in almost all his patients who wiped their noses just after seizures. "Surprisingly, the hand a person uses to wipe his or her nose correlates with the same side of the body a seizure originates," said Baumgartner.

Chapter 5

Treatment

After making the diagnosis, the doctor must decide on the best treatment. There are many options available today. In the past, people turned to magic spells or prayer to treat epilepsy. Ancient Greek doctors told their patients to drink wine mixed with powdered human skull. During Galen's time, the Romans tried putting blood on the lips of a person having an attack.

Frogs' Livers and Human Skulls

During the Middle Ages, other strange treatments for epilepsy were used. Doctors gave patients drugs made from mistletoe, dogs' blood, frog's liver, or human urine. Some thought that wearing a necklace of chrysanthemums and peonies would help. In drastic cases, doctors cut or burned holes in the patient's skull, "to let out the 'mischievous matter' that was causing the problem." Arab doctors of this time used a treatment that worked for some patients, a diet high in fat. Even today, doctors sometimes prescribe a special diet—called a **ketogenic diet**—that is high in fat and low in protein and carbohydrates for patients who have seizures.

The first important advance in epilepsy treatment occurred in the 1850s. An English doctor, Sir Charles Locock, prescribed potassium bromide for his epilepsy patients. Doctors had been giving this sedative to people with nervous problems for some time. In most cases, the drug stopped all seizures. However, there were serious side effects. People taking the sedative sometimes became confused and their health deteriorated. In some cases the drug caused serious mental problems.

Today's Medicines

In 1912 German doctor Alfred Hauptmann found a better medicine for epilepsy—phenobarbital. It prevented seizures in many people and caused few side effects. The widespread use of phenobarbital led to a change in public attitudes about epilepsy. People with epilepsy could lead normal lives, and many were able to avoid seizures altogether.

More progress in epilepsy treatment came in 1938 when Dr. Tracey J. Putnam tested different medications on cats. He induced seizures in the animals' brains by applying electric shocks. If the medicine stopped the seizure, he increased the voltage of the shock. Putnam found that phenytoin stopped seizures at much higher voltages than phenobarbital, and it didn't put the cat to sleep. Until then, doctors had thought the sedative effect of phenobarbital might be what prevented seizures. Phenytoin, sold as

Dilantin, continues to be one of the most prescribed medicines for epilepsy. Carbamazapine and valproate are other medicines commonly prescribed to people who have just been diagnosed with epilepsy. Doctors still prescribe phenobarbital for some people. Other common epilepsy medicines include clonazepam and primidone.

Today there are more than twenty medications to treat epilepsy. Scientists don't really know just how the medications work. Some prevent seizures; others reduce the severity of the seizures. A doctor chooses the medication that has worked best for most people with the same symptoms as those of the patient. If the medication doesn't work or has unpleasant side effects, the doctor tries something else. Sometimes patients take more than one medication to stop the seizures.

They may also take other medications to reduce side effects. Side effects include nausea, dizziness, sleepiness, skin rashes, blurred vision, and slurred speech. Sometimes, medications make it hard to do well in school or make behavior problems more likely. Several of the newer medicines have fewer side effects than the older drugs or may be more effective for some types of epilepsy. Some can be injected if the patient cannot swallow the medication in pill form.

Tamara experienced side effects when she took medication to treat her epilepsy. "It was harder to lose fat, my skin was sallow and looked unhealthy...I got sick easier, [and] I was exhausted," she said. "When I cut myself, the blood took longer to clot. I scarred more easily and from more minor wounds than I ever had." David Hall said the medicine he takes makes his gums bleed easily.

Doctors carefully monitor patients who are taking epilepsy medicine. The dosage must be built up slowly to a level that will control seizures. Higher levels can be poisonous, causing serious side effects. Blood samples are drawn and analyzed at regular intervals. Once the levels of medicine in the blood are the same for a period of weeks, the doctor and the patient decide whether the medication is working. If it is not, the doctor slowly reduces the dosage. Then the patient tries a new medication. Since people react to medicines differently, it may take years to find the best treatment for a particular person. New drugs are developed every year. One new medicine is being made from tarantula venom, which changes the brain chemistry.

Various things can interfere with the effectiveness of a medicine. Medications used for other health problems can react badly with the medicine. So can alcohol or illegal drugs. Sometimes the combination of illegal drugs or alcohol and the medicine cause dangerous side effects. Or the drugs and alcohol stop the medicine from working correctly. Poor diet can also interfere with the effectiveness of a medicine. Age can be a factor. For example, during puberty, hormones are released into the bloodstream that may affect how well a medicine works.

Proper medicines control epilepsy in about 80 percent of people with the disorder. Their seizures are reduced to manageable levels. About half of the people being treated for epilepsy will never have another seizure as long as they take their medicine. Doctors and patients must balance the benefit of controlling seizures against the bad effects of medicines. Sometimes it is better to accept an occasional seizure rather than risk dangerous side effects.

Vagus Nerve Stimulator

One of the newest methods for dealing with epilepsy is the **vagus nerve stimulator (VNS)**. The vagus nerve connects the brain to the body's major organs. Doctors have found that electric stimulation of the vagus nerve sometimes stops seizures. Surgeons implant a VNS generator and battery in the chest. An electrical lead feeds under the skin to connect with the vagus nerve in the neck. The VNS works like a pacemaker. Pacemakers are implanted devices that have been used for decades to control heart problems.

Doctors program the VNS with a special magnet held next to the skin near the generator. They set the VNS to deliver a small electrical charge at preset times. A typical "dose" is thirty seconds every five minutes. Patients can also use a magnet to operate the VNS manually, if they sense a seizure is coming. The VNS works automatically for many years. Every five years or so, minor surgery is needed to replace the battery.

When the charge is on, the patient may cough or feel a slight discomfort in the throat. There may be some shortness of breath. A person's voice may change. VNS treatment has no mental side effects as some medications do. There is little or no pain.

The VNS will not cure epilepsy. Doctors implant the device only if medications don't work well. Most patients find that the VNS gradually reduces the number and sometimes the strength of seizures. Some patients report that they sense auras more easily with the VNS. This gives them time to prepare for a seizure.

Ketogenic Diet

Some children can control their epilepsy by eating a ketogenic diet. They eat food high in fat and low in protein and carbohydrates. Patients on the ketogenic diet must be careful to monitor what and how much they eat. When a person limits carbohydrates, the body burns fat for energy instead of glucose. Glucose is a simple sugar derived from carbohydrates and normally used by the body to produce energy. When the body burns fat, a substance called ketones, or acid wastes, is produced.

Russell Wilder developed the ketogenic diet in the 1920s. Wilder thought that ketones, produced in the blood during fasts, helped stop seizures. He developed a nutritious diet that caused the body to produce ketones. The diet works best for children who have generalized seizures. Two-thirds of children with epilepsy who are on a ketogenic diet reduce their number of seizures. One of three may never have another attack. Children on the diet must be checked regularly by a doctor.

Alternative Treatments

Medicines do not work for everyone with epilepsy. Such people look for other ways to ease their symptoms. One way is to reduce or eliminate things that bring on seizures. Stress is often a factor in triggering seizures. There are many ways to reduce stress. Meditation is a mental exercise to calm the mind. Many patients report success with this method. Some patients lie in a darkened room and concentrate on a candle flame. Some repeat a nonsense phrase.

Others practice deep-breathing exercises. Many people benefit from yoga or other regular exercise. Another method of relaxing is self-hypnosis, in which people begin to relax as they tell themselves repeatedly that they are calm.

A patient monitors his brain activity, using a biofeedback machine. The screen on the right records the patient's brain waves as he plays a computer game designed for use in biofeedback.

People with epilepsy can sometimes reduce seizures through a process known as **biofeedback**. This technique relies on machines to tell people what their bodies are doing. For instance, stress often raises blood pressure. By watching a monitor that is connected to one of the wrists, a person can see on a chart or video screen whether the blood pressure is rising or falling. Then he or she practices various methods of reducing stress to find one that lowers the blood pressure.

Besides teaching people how to reduce stress, biofeedback can help treat epilepsy directly. Patients can see and hear the strength and rhythm of their brain waves by watching a monitor connected to an electroencephalograph. Some patients can learn to alter their brain waves this way.

Dr. Maurice Sterman was the first to discover that such training can affect epileptic seizures. He trained cats to produce a particular pattern of brain waves called **sensorimotor rhythm (SMR)**. An SMR pattern helps reduce seizures. Whenever the cats' EEGs showed the SMR pattern, Dr. Sterman rewarded them with food. Later, he gave the cats a medication that caused seizures. The cats that had been trained to produce SMR brain waves had fewer seizures than the cats without the training.

Dr. Sterman then trained humans who had epilepsy to produce SMR brain waves. The number of seizures decreased in these people. Since those experiments, many people with epilepsy have learned to control their brain waves. They use various mental techniques to do so. During her SMR training, Sally Fletcher found that she needed to do the following to produce SMR waves: "[I] needed to concentrate on something very intently, with my eyes open, such as doing multiplication, thinking of a sequence or pattern of numbers, visualizing certain scenes, or imagining that I was reading some words or music."

Some people can prevent seizures by practicing SMR training techniques when they have an aura. Others who produce SMR waves regularly have found that they have fewer attacks as time goes on. And this method has no side effects. SMR training is not a substitute for effective medication. It doesn't work for many people with epilepsy. But for a few people, it is the only hope.

Surgery—A Last Resort

Surgery is an option for a few people with epilepsy. Because brain surgery is so dangerous, a doctor will consider it only if the patient doesn't respond to medicines or other treatment. Surgery can be performed only on patients with focal epilepsy. The surgery involves cutting out a small area of the brain where the seizures start. The surgeon operates only if this won't interfere with other brain functions. Surgery is becoming more common today as doctors improve their techniques.

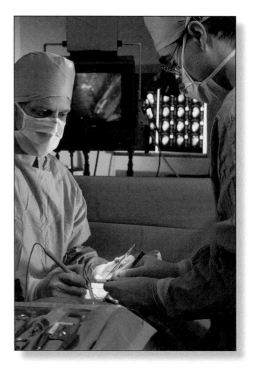

Doctors must be able to locate the exact position of the focal point. Before surgery, the patient is attached to an electroencephalograph, and an EEG records seizures constantly for several days. MRIs and CAT scans help find the

A surgeon operates on a patient's brain.

focal point of the seizures. Sometimes the patient can assist in locating the focal point. Because brains have no feeling, patients are often awake during brain surgery. The doctor stimulates an area of the brain with an electric probe. If the patient feels the warning signs of an aura, he tells the doctor. The surgeon then knows that spot is the focal point. Surgery doesn't always work. Sometimes the operation leaves a scar that becomes a new focal point.

People with epilepsy sometimes stop having seizures for no known reason. In many of these cases, symptoms disappear mysteriously by the time a person reaches the mid-twenties. As in the case of Tamara Moxham, these people have what is known as childhood epilepsy.

Chapter 6

Living With Epilepsy

A lthough the days when people with epilepsy were chained in asylums are gone, these people still have social and legal battles to win. For example, as recently as 1982, some states still had laws on record that banned people with epilepsy from marrying. These laws were passed to discourage people from having children who might also have epilepsy. However, people with epilepsy are only slightly more likely than other people to have children with the disorder. Even if the risk were greater, however, many people contend that a state should not have the right to say who should and should not marry.

Discrimination against people with epilepsy takes other forms, too. Some employers are reluctant to hire people with epilepsy. Job applications used to have the question "Do you have epilepsy?" The Americans with Disabilities Act, passed by Congress in 1990, forbids employers from asking that question or others like it.

The reluctance to hire people with epilepsy persists.

Employers fear that people with epilepsy will hurt themselves on the job. In fact, studies show that people with epilepsy have fewer accidents and are more productive than other workers.

A quarter of the people with epilepsy in the United States are unemployed. Many of those who do work are qualified for better jobs. Tamara Moxham recalled, "I was hurried out of job interviews when it came up that I had a history of seizures, even when the seizures wouldn't have affected my job performance."

Problems and Challenges

People with epilepsy face other problems and challenges. Many states used to deny anyone with epilepsy a driver's license. Most states now require a doctor's note before they will issue a driver's license to someone with epilepsy. People must show that they have not had seizures for a period of time, usually a year. People with epilepsy pay higher rates for both car and medical insurance. People with epilepsy also have problems getting hunting or fishing licenses.

Daily life has many challenges for anyone with epilepsy. For example, it is inconvenient not to be able to drive. Many people with epilepsy must avoid concerts that have strobe lights. Even in the safety of a person's home, there are problems. The flickering of a television set can start an attack for some. People who have epilepsy sometimes sleep without pillows. They are afraid that during a seizure they may push their faces into their pillows and suffocate.

"Seizure dogs" help some people with epilepsy. Just as

Tamara Moxham pictured in 1999 when she was twenty-nine. Diagnosed with childhood epilepsy, she no longer has to take medicine to control seizures.

guide dogs assist blind people, seizure dogs are trained to alert others and protect the person who is having a seizure. Some people report that their dogs can somehow sense when a seizure is coming and warn their owners.

Women with epilepsy must be extra careful during pregnancy. Seizures or the medications used to prevent them can endanger an unborn child or cause birth defects or miscarriages. Infants who were exposed to medications in the womb may have to go through withdrawal after they are born. Breastfeeding may be dangerous because of the traces of medications in the mother's milk. Even so, more than 95 percent of women with epilepsy who give birth have normal babies and no problems with delivery.

Some children who have epilepsy develop learning problems. This may be a result of frequent absence attacks that occur while the teacher is explaining the lesson. Or a child's epilepsy medicine may make him or her less alert. In other children, seizures may affect the ability to remember. On average, children with epilepsy tend to be one year behind the expected reading level.

Seizures themselves are rarely life-threatening, but their effects can be dangerous. People who have generalized seizures are especially at risk. There is always the risk of falling and hurting oneself. In severe cases, children must wear protective helmets whenever there is a chance they may fall. A blow to the head can worsen their epilepsy.

Danger lurks in many places for people who have seizures. They must avoid high places. They go swimming only with friends nearby. Some people who have epilepsy take showers instead of baths because they fear drowning during a seizure. An attack that occurs while the person is driving can be fatal.

People sometimes treat those with epilepsy unfairly. Some teachers believe students who have absence seizures aren't paying attention in class. Children sometimes make fun of another child who behaves oddly during a temporal lobe seizure. Often, people treat anyone with a brain disease as stupid. "When some people learned that I had epilepsy," Tamara Moxham said, "they talked to me slowly, assuming that because epilepsy affects the brain, I wasn't smart enough to understand what they were saying."

People who have epilepsy often have poor self-images. One parent said, "My son won't admit to anyone that he has epilepsy because he thinks anyone who knows will look down on him or make fun of him." This can lead to depression or anger, which can make epilepsy worse. About 20 percent of those with epilepsy become depressed.

Besides having to deal with the hardships of the illness itself, people who have epilepsy may worry that they will never recover nor be able to lead a normal life. They also must face prejudice from others who don't understand the facts about epilepsy. People who have seizures in public may feel that they have lost their dignity. Often, seizures are harder on family members and friends than on the person having the attack. One parent said of her son, "When he has a seizure, if I try to touch him to comfort him, he doesn't respond. He is so alone. I can't get through. I have to stand and just watch him, and there is just nothing I can do to make it stop."

Famous People With Epilepsy

Recent studies have shown that epilepsy has no effect on intelligence. Many of history's greatest figures had the disorder. Epilepsy didn't keep Alexander the Great from conquering the vast Persian Empire more than two thousand years ago. Julius Caesar, the greatest of the ancient Roman emperors, had epilepsy. So did famous classical music composers Wolfgang Amadeus Mozart, George Frederick Handel, and Peter Ilich Tchaikovsky.

Great writers who had epilepsy include Lord Byron, Charles Dickens, and Dante. Artists Vincent van Gogh and Leonardo da Vinci had the disorder. Pope Pius IX had epilepsy. So did Buddha, spiritual leader of millions of Buddhists. It is believed that Mohammed, founder of the Muslim faith, also had epilepsy.

What People Can Do to Help

Better education is slowly erasing the stigma of epilepsy. Medical experts and members of the general public are learning that those with epilepsy are no more likely to commit crimes than other people. Doctors and teachers now avoid describing a seizure as a "fit," which makes a seizure sound like a temper tantrum. Doctors encourage people with epilepsy to participate in sports and lead active lives. Activists are working to repeal laws that discriminate against those with epilepsy. Support groups, such as the Epilepsy Foundation of America, help many people with the disorder.

People with epilepsy should not be treated like invalids. It's also important to know what to do if a person has an attack. There is no way to stop a seizure once it has begun. A person having a temporal lobe seizure should be left alone unless he or she is in danger. If a person has a generalized seizure, bystanders can ease the person gently down to the ground. When a person has a tonic-clonic attack, dangerous objects should be removed from the area.

People once believed that a person having a seizure might swallow his or her tongue. They forced something into the mouth of the person having a seizure to prevent him or her from choking. But this does more harm than good. Forcing something into a person's mouth can cause the person to choke. People having a seizure may bite their tongues, but it is impossible to swallow the tongue.

Bystanders should not try to keep a person from shaking during a seizure. If the person's head is banging on the floor, someone can use his or her hands or a pillow to cushion the blows. Once the shaking stops, the person's head can be turned gently to the side so saliva won't flow into the windpipe and cause choking. The person should not be moved; waking up in a different position can be confusing. Usually, medical attention is not needed immediately, although the person should check with his or her doctor after the episode. In rare cases, a person may have repeated seizures. Whenever a person has trouble breathing for more than a few minutes, medical attention is needed right away. If the attack goes on for more than five minutes, the person should be taken to the hospital immediately.

Once a person regains consciousness, he or she should rest quietly. A person who has just had a seizure may be confused. The person may need someone to explain what has happened. Someone should stay with the person until he or she recovers.

Tamara Moxham advises, "The best help you can be is to make sure the person does not wake up to a crowd of people staring at him or her. This is embarrassing, and it is totally unnecessary to have a group of people standing around. If people begin to stop, quietly tell them that a person is having a seizure and that it is being handled, and then try to convince them to leave."

Those with epilepsy should try to remember that people are curious about anything unusual. They shouldn't feel picked on. Almost everyone has some special problem. Some problems are more serious than others. It is important for people with epilepsy to educate themselves about the disorder and to teach others that epilepsy is no reason for fear or scorn.

Most of all, those with epilepsy shouldn't lose hope. About 80 percent of people with epilepsy can successfully be treated for the disorder. They almost never have seizures after receiving treatment. Medical research continues, and scientists discover better treatments every year. With advances in research, treatment, and information, the future looks brighter for those with epilepsy everywhere.

Further Reading

Carson, Mary Kay. *Epilepsy (Diseases and People)*.
Berkeley Heights, N.J.: Enslow Publishers, Inc., 1998.

Devinsky, Orrin. *A Guide to Understanding and Living
With Epilepsy*. Philadelphia: F.A. Davis Co., 1994.

Epilepsy Foundation of America. *The Legal Rights of
Persons with Epilepsy*. Landover, Md., 1992.

Epilepsy Foundation of America. *Facts About Epilepsy*.
Landover, Md., 1990.

Freeman, John, Millicent Kelly, and Jennifer Freeman.
*The Epilepsy Diet Treatment: An Introduction To The
Ketogenic Diet*. New York: Demos Publications, 1994.

Freeman, J.M., E.P.G. Vining, and D.J. Pillas. *Seizures
and Epilepsy in Childhood: A Guide for Parents*.
Baltimore, Md.: Johns Hopkins Press, 1997.

Gumnit, Robert J. *Living Well With Epilepsy*. New York:
Demos Vermande Publications, 1997.

Jan, J.E., R.G. Ziegler, and G. Erba. *Does Your Child Have
Epilepsy?* Austin, Texas: Austin Pro-Ed Press, 1991.

Landau, Elaine. *Epilepsy (Understanding Illness)*. New
York: Twenty-First Century Books, 1995.

Richard, A. and J. Reiter. *Epilepsy: A New Approach*. New
York: Prentice Hall Press, 1990.

Schachter, Steven. *Brainstorms—Epilepsy In Our Words:
Personal Accounts of Living With Seizures*. New York:
Raven Press, 1993.

For More Information

The following is a list of resources that deal with epilepsy.

Organizations

Citizens United for Research in Epilepsy (CURE)
8110 Woodside Lane, Burr Ridge IL 60525; (630) 734-9957/(630) 734-9964; <http://www.CUREepilepsy.org>

Epilepsy Canada
1470 Peel Street, Suite 745, Montreal, Quebec H3A 1T1; (514)845-7855 or (800) 860-5499; <http://www.epilepsy.ca>

Epilepsy Foundation of America
4351 Garden City Drive, Landover, MD 20785; (800) 332-1000, (301) 459-3700; <http://www.efa.org>

National Institute of Neurological Disorders and Stroke
Office of Communications & Public Liaison, P.O. Box 5801, Bethesda, MD 20824; (301) 496-4000; <http://www.ninds.nih.gov/health_and_medical/disorders/epilepsy.htm>

Internet Resources

<http://kidshealth.org>
KidsHealth, run by The Nemours Foundation.

<http://www.aafp.org/patientinfo/epilepsy.html>
Site of the American Academy of Family Physicians.

<http://www.drkoop.com/conditions/Epilepsy>
Site of C. Everett Koop, former U.S. Surgeon General.

Glossary

absence seizure—A generalized seizure in which a person briefly loses consciousness, but without falling.

akinetic seizure—A generalized seizure in which a person briefly stops moving.

Alzheimer's disease—A disease of the brain affecting the elderly that can increase the chances of having epilepsy.

atonic seizure—A generalized seizure in which a person briefly loses muscle control and falls.

auditory cortex—The brain part that controls hearing.

aura—The sensation sometimes felt before a seizure.

autonomic nervous system—The part of the nervous system controlling involuntary functions such as heart rate.

autonomic seizure—A partial seizure that affects the autonomic nervous system.

axon—The stem-like part of a neuron that sends an electric signal to the next cell.

biofeedback—A training method using medical equipment that helps a person to regulate body functions.

brain wave—The pattern of electrical signals sent out by the brain.

clonic phase—The second stage of tonic-clonic seizures in which the muscles jerk.

complex partial seizure—A partial seizure in which a person's consciousness is affected.

computerized axial tomography (CAT)—A medical test that shows pictures of internal body parts.

dendrite—The branch-like part of a neuron that receives electric signals.

electroencephalogram (EEG)—The record of brain waves made by an electroencephalograph.

electroencephalograph—A medical device that records brain waves.

focal point—The part of the brain where a seizure starts.

generalized seizure—A seizure affecting the whole brain.

idiopathic epilepsy—Epilepsy that has no known cause.

Jacksonian epilepsy—A type of epilepsy in which a motor seizure moves along the length of an arm or leg.

ketogenic diet—A low-protein, low-carbohydrate, high-fat diet helpful in reducing seizures in some children.

kindling—The process in which the brain learns to repeat previous electrical discharges.

magnetic resonance imaging (MRI)—A medical test using magnetic signals to show the internal organs.

magnetoencephalogram (MEG)–A medical test that uses magnetic fields to show brain structures.

motor seizure—A partial seizure that affects only muscles.

myoclonic seizure—A generalized seizure that causes the muscles to shake.

neurologist—A doctor who specializes in the brain and nervous system.

neuron—Nerve cells; they send information throughout the body by electrical signals.

neurotransmitter—A chemical that sends signals from the axon to the dendrite.

partial seizure—A seizure in which the electrical discharge is confined to a small part of the brain. Only the part of the body controlled by that area is affected.

positron emission tomography (PET)—A test that uses radioactive dye to show internal body parts at work.

precipitant—Anything that triggers an epileptic seizure.

pseudo seizure—A seizure caused by psychological problems, not epilepsy.

psychic seizure—A partial seizure affecting the emotions.

secondarily generalized seizure—A seizure that begins as a partial seizure and leads to a generalized seizure.

seizure—A sudden electrical discharge in the brain that upsets normal brain functions.

sensorimotor rhythm (SMR)—A certain type of brain wave pattern that is associated with fewer seizures.

sensory seizure—A partial seizure that causes a person to see, hear, smell, taste, or feel things that aren't real.

simple partial seizure—A seizure which affects simple muscles but does not result in loss of consciousness.

single photon emission computed tomography (SPECT)– A test that locates the focal points of seizures.

status epilepticus—A life-threatening condition in which a person has continuous seizures.

symptomatic epilepsy—Epilepsy that has a known cause.

temporal lobe—The part of the brain controlling speech, sensation, and consciousness.

tonic phase—The first stage of tonic-clonic seizures in which the muscles become rigid.

tonic-clonic seizure—A generalized seizure in which the muscles first go rigid, then jerk.

vagus nerve stimulator (VNS)—A device put in the chest that stimulates the vagus nerve and helps control seizures. The vagus nerve connects the brain to the body's major organs.

Index